WHEN PERFORMERS SWIM, THE DICE ARE CAST

Poems by
Judy Katz-Levine

8-9-16

ahadada
books
tokyo / toronto

General Editor: Jesse Glass
Layout and design: Joe Zanghi, Printed Matter Press
Cover photo: Joe Zanghi
Photograph of the author: Barry I. Levine

editorial address:

3158 Bentworth Drive
Burlington, Ontario
Canada L7M-1M2

Emergency Editions
First Edition
Printed and Bound in Canada

ISBN 978-0-9811704-3-5

Acknowledgements

The author wishes to gratefully acknowledge the following magazines in which some of these poems appeared:

Salamander: "She Speaks Of Horses"

The Delinquent: "On Mortality", "Gifts", "Redemptions", "she has said..."

Istanbul Literary Review: "Poem Written At Night, April", "Reading Bialik By Rainlight", "A Spark, A Vision", "Performers"

New Verse News: "Blood Storms"

The Aurorean: "the dynamics of August"

Grateful acknowledgement and gracious thanks are made by the author to the following subscribers:

Jenny Barber, poet, editor of "Salamander"
Paul Roth, poet, editor of "The Bitter Oleander"
Mark Pawlak, poet, editor of "Hanging Loose"
Edith Levine
Barry Levine

POEMS

ON MORTALITY

you could be anywhere. but you're here in the room. don't turn your back. wait. there are possibilities still with us. and possibilities estranged. not rainfall & ravens. instead, a current of electricity. magnets explained by an adolescent. this young man whoops it up over the universe's peculiarities. then he doesn't eat. you and i, we talk about what's hard to talk about. mortality whispers in the night rain. the will to survive emerges. our car with dim headlights still runs. we hear the swish of cars on the highway. living symbols—your hands that fix computers...the lily on the young man's computer screen

CROWS

they are at the periphery
of my vision. they call
in a language that penetrates
the leaves, turning now
oh ochre & maroon
the ships of the yards
quiver, the limbs of the trees
shake their tresses
the crows observe
as I observe, breath
becomes the one constant
as the blue tent of sky
tent of the ancients
becomes one with the cars
and I become one with a soul
I've never heard before
name is invisible

I GET BY

I get by. When having a glass of wine, I get stern. My doctor says I shouldn't drink at all. And what with all the medicine I take, sterner still. The drummer was playing a fast marimba beat to a slow sad ballad and I got off, got in a good solo. There's a wet snow today as I remember. It's almost stopped. So many yellow leaves, & the stars. I've had a revelation. Seagulls float. The sax was smooth, delicious as a chili with wine. The guitarist did tasty licks from his days on the road. This was at the party. The drummer, a woman, said "Sometimes you just have to shake your money-maker" and did a little shimmy behind her drums and grinned. I loosened up. Laughed.

PERFORMERS

when performers swim, the dice are cast. sounds like a piano doing ragtime, echo of the voice of a clown across the sea.

when performers laugh, the trees whistle as if hearing. jugglers on sand dunes remember.

when performers tango, stages turn into bridges. an aster in a garden blooms.

when performers teach, a taut drum vibrates. a Native American flute holds its breath, then come the long notes haunting an audience.

when performers die, the oceans leap up and keen as seals emerge and fly.

REDEMPTIONS

1

I lose my place playing flute in the samba. The trees quiver in brief wind. A hot winter. Rain. When looking out the window sable scarves. Losing one's place is like tripping, not falling. The pianist grins. We go on to another tune, "Corcovado", and I redeem myself.

2

Day of gifts like blue hydrangea. I remember a grandfather who loved to fix watches—the gears in the jars. You empty a jar of screws you use to fix your sax mouthpiece. Enlightened look on your face as you concentrate, barely noticing my presence, my ego lit up by a new book.

3

Tired after listening, we sleep. I dream of my mother, having a party. For this one she has two plump helpers. There are my brothers. She takes a photo of them standing together, but refuses to take one of me. Then she relents, after teasing me this way, and snaps.

GIFTS

4 pots of chrysanthemums, magenta, bathe
in sunlight, myriad buds bend and open

basil leaves, their fragrance, from which
I make a pesto, sharp and tangy with garlic

not to mention the spearmint
which we'll plant—sits now in the refrigerator

rootlets will come

and an enormous bag of ripe cherry tomatoes
and the beet greens & beets

the greens which we fried up with onions
had with a curried omelet

the beets from which we'll make a borscht
with potato and an egg

and the walking by dry grass of an autumn parched
in the park where oaks turn ochre & saffron

FRINGED GARMENT THAT LEADS TO A PERSON

One person leads to another and to another
Dressed as a mime, playing drums & flute
in the square, I in a red-striped jersey and jeans—beret—
when he came, holding flowers, also dressed
as a mime, in white face, when strangers were passing.

And the sun gave us a strange light
like the light in a clearing in
the woods
of New Jersey, where sassafras undergrowth exists
and I thought of him there when we were kids—

But the white glare of the sun
now as I awaken 15 years later
reminds me of a man in shredded garments
face chalk-white so long ago, eyes black, black hair
coming up from a shaved head like grass
standing in the sun
before he fell

SHE SPEAKS OF HORSES

after Georg Trakl

She speaks of horses, she speaks of hours.
The enormous eyes of the horses, how
they bend their heads when hunger gnaws.

The light tonight is dismal, suffused.
A sabbath without answers
as the trees crystalize in rain.

Who will I meet, what stranger, emerging
from the dark wells of the eyes of those horses
what body lit under a midnight crescent?

Beds of hyacinths breathe and sway
Beds of aging women who dwell in gifts of the spirit

The horses moan as lightning ceases

WANG WEI

An ice storm today, the sky breathes snow.
The twigs of the trees shine against pearl grays.
I read the poet Wang Wei, read about his life
in the government, his skill as a musician.
There's a brushstroke painting of him on my computer
playing an instrument like a zither—maybe he also
played the Chinese lute—pipa.
I wonder if I've ever had a life
in a monastery, creating
calligraphy of waterfalls and birds,
strolling alone to a mountain cave
where the moss glistens under the moon.

WISHBONES OF TREES

Wishbones of trees
humble as the holy

One raven traverses the drifts

Crescent moon aura

evening
a coyote loose in the city

growling sax
pleads a bluesy riff

light two candles

dream—
walking with her over a field
my teacher

ONE FOR RYU

He sent me a concert poster of a woman, a Japanese
musician—Nishimatsu Fuei —holding what looks
like a Japanese banjo. Sent me a card
of a Chassid playing a cello, sent me
books and books and books, some
of his own, some by poets he published, one
on Emily Dickinson, sent me a tape of Native
American flute music, and myriad letters.
Over twenty years, we sat down together three times.

His phone number is disconnected. He is at
Convalescent hospital, and cannot be reached.
My publisher, he traveled to Japan, China,
Europe, Israel, and wrote with little recognition. Just as
his press was becoming well known, he tripped
and fell hard and I cannot reach out to him...

A SPARK, A VISION

Ravens came today.
I mailed a letter, drove
into town. Now a saxophone, now
a poem about the Spanish Civil War
by Machado:

"The mother, her forehead dark
between a day gone and a day to come,
sees a fire nearly out
and an oven with spiders".*

Now a correspondence.

The dog next door
ran into our yard, threatening
my husband's patients.

I made a soup from chicken bones,
with barley, shitake mushrooms, kale.

I heard a voice: " You had another life
in the Shoah, you were a little girl
brought to the slaughter..."

I saw a vision - a spark of blue light.
A man in a fur hat surrounded by a halo.

I didn't tell a soul.

*from the poem "Rainbow At Night" translated by Robert Bly,
from the book "Against Forgetting" edited by Carolyn Forche

BLOOD STORMS

they say a storm will come. e-mail the whitehouse on Darfur, imagine what a young girl suffers in a camp in Darfur as the snow starts to fall.
to be raped as a child. that innocent and wounded. to be that hungry to starve. the whitehouse e-mails me back immediately with a form letter. every night we hear about the limbs of soldiers maimed, Iraqis killed.

the news is a horror show. there's blood on the table. there's blood on the dishrags. our ears are covered in blood, blood in the snow. politicians plead for votes, as the ice storms rage. it is the ice of a country numbed by war. the face of a child in Darfur a sign of the prophet. no more. no more blood storms.

POEM WRITTEN AT NIGHT, APRIL

A dog howls in the night.
Rain, then it ceases.

Forsythia burn like lamps, days.
A raven, my friend, flies to the high oak.
Perches there, overseer of cars & avenues.

A new planet is discovered.
This young man, curious, thinks
there may be life therein. Granite, even
water, the heaviest of gravity, maybe life
on another planet, after all.

SUNSET II

Alone in a room, I have a hunch, a message.
Clowning around, my son talks about sci-fi, authors.
At dawn—birds, you next to me, I worrying.
Actual facts rain down.
Last night's love making
earthy and Kama Sutra-like.
Obelisks in a teacher's vision.
Dusk, my son and I speak of Hamlet, that his life
had meaning. My son lifts
his hands for emphasis.

SUNSET III

trees with leaves like the hands of prodigies.
a boat still in twilight, in the neighbor's driveway.
a son about to redeem himself.
lilac with 9 unripe flowers.
saxophone moaning its scales, ready to play Monk's
"Ruby My Dear".
prodigies who can't control their thirst for knowledge.
prodigies who can't fit in, and talk strange languages.
prodigies who wait for the morning's river.
being 4 years old that time of glistening forsythia.
being 4 years old that time of grandpa's lap and the watch he fixed
just before he never came back.
being 4 years old and speaking perfectly.
saxophone mourning its scales like burning lilacs, ready to play
"The Night Has A Thousand Eyes".
saxophone twittering its soprano notes as dusk flies in.
decisions to make. oh the many decisions as dusk flies in.
a boat in dry dock but someday it will float.
a boat in dry dock by the house catching last light.
a boat not quite ready, but we are patiently waiting for that day.

THE ATTRIBUTES

the attributes of this saintly presence are to be numbered according to flowers. the initiate will enumerate laughter. according to myths and waterfalls; giant spiders, miners lost in mines due to seismic tremors. what is lost, and what can be seen—the white circle above, the woods below. the air caressing the spruce and moths in circles above the grass, a dog barks. this breathing will announce an arrival.

THE DYNAMICS OF AUGUST

a lanky young man.
a dog who comes up to me in the park, harmless.
the car, its sheen on the way to the lake.
a runner, her sleek figure. a walker on a cell phone.
in the limpid green water friends everywhere stand in
luminous light.
a sadness—the moth's crying silent prayer—it is myself.

WAYS OF BEING

Uncanny smiles turn towards snow-light.
Breach of waves in dream.
There were dances, the whales bounced.
Acquire the face of an angel.
winnowing hats. A baseball cap.
Small wooden flutes, a photograph.
Three cups coffee.
An avocado ripens.
Be particular about voice...open the throat
with a yawn, then let the sound fly.

Continue with a samba, that fast.

The bass holds time, a watch of pearls. The drummer has
many clicking stories.

If I could remember my past, all would be photographs.
No wind today, but a raw April. To write it down with a sip,
a sigh.

CHOIR TEXTS

1

A Mentor

you were interested in me, in my voice.
and the night cascaded.
you blessed me with your voice
and the afternoon grew a bamboo flute.
you held your self discretely aware,
yet remained open as a field.
this was your job.
you basically sang, and sang, and sang.
I came forth, taking on the task of singing.
I learned to sing as a steady alto.
even when dizzy on stage, I held on.
now we have another year to go.
I think of the ocean,
a ride on a ferry at sunset,
all glorious...

2

CHOIR TEXT 1

my friend has an answer.
sequestered.
choir me.
the apples are tart.
elongated tongues,
notes of the tenor rise & reach.
an inexplicable serene nodding of the head.
my friend has answered me
not only with music but with words.
stark are the trees.
my friend reaches for your hand's voice.
an alluvial piece, this,
like a rivering arm with ripples, conducts.
this is the power that is restrained
like closed eyes when singing.
breathe.
then take in the jumping
of piano pianissimo pianissimo a quiet
sequestered. to believe

CHOIR TEXT 2

you choir me into serving.
the voices blend & tigerlily run.
black orchids are notes precisely placed in time.
hyacinths are the given unerring understanding text
of systems & musical notations.
choir constellations.
faces & bodies sway or stand sturdy.
follow the ascending line,
the descending to low bass & tenor years yearning to keep time.
wells of restraint well up
emotional notebooks forever young.

AMHERST, MA 6-15-07

The Berkshires, mountains.
A cheap motel, university
of youths, an old friend, we meet
in town—a musician who plays
blues & sings with a gritty bass, sings
Hindu sutras, too, chants
for followers—says
"yes don't we look old, "talks of
a battle with diabetes

I dream
my cousin, her mother, a hill
luminescent—

in the afternoon you play
your sax
by the parking lot, under a grove
of pines, the soprano, a Bach.

Our son is attending an orientation
for university life. We see him once
during these three days, he's
eating pepperoni pizza.

The air
alternately blazing & cool here by the pines
where you play. This morning Tai Chi
by a park, not quite an Eden, but with
a small creek, & earlier, walking a path
we came to a wild rose bush & the scent
of wild roses.

READING BIALIK BY RAINLIGHT

His poem about an embrace, his
writing on a steel gray morning
in Russia, God's creation. I
pick up the guitar, play a nigun
by Carlebach, a wedding tune
a ballad of sorts. The rain
and steel gray of sky
just like Bialik said
in Ashkenazic Hebrew, permeates
the afternoon, and the sound
of rain against the windows
not like in Tel Aviv
which I have never visited,
not even in dreams
though I did have one
about a rabbi the other night.
She did go to Israel.
I saw her photo there
in the newsletter,
and she asked me, in the dream
questions about my health.
Bialik died in Vienna
being treated for a medical problem.
I don't know much about Bialik
only this poem about the steel gray sky
in Russia, and the one about
an embrace, like two trees
in a solitary world.

(I WAS) A YEMENITE WOMAN

I was Yemenite woman, a Jew in Yemen
who danced under the stars. And sang
to myself, hearing the wind
through the grasses of marshes
and the ringing and bell-like melodies
of handmade instruments of metal.
I had goats, and cured people with herbs
found in the highlands. My ancestors came
with King Solomon's craftsmen, merchants,
and with the prophet Jeremiah.
They learned to use rue and henna
for weddings, rue to ward off evil, henna a call
to The Beloved. I had a son. People came
to him to be blessed—to receive
teachings, and he could read though
I couldn't. I danced a hop and a step, then
a sideways step. Three steps at a time,
as we were forbidden to dance freely. And
as I danced, my son read
in Hebrew, and in Aramaic,
the ancient holy texts like the branches of apricot trees
against the sky and the patterns
of sandstone on our walls.

SONG WITH DARKNESS & LIGHT, MARCH

The trees are barren, but earnestly want to bud.
A woman earnestly wants to be one with me in prayer and song.
A raven lights down on the straw of a yard across the street.
This woman nods her head towards me, calming me.
A young man comes home with subterranean stories.
Someone on his campus has been knifed, someone beaten.
He tells me of psychopaths, he's struggling.
The rose in my meditation is hidden, then apparent, etched.
I only want to think of a jazz pianist, birthing whole tone chords in
the rustle of March wind. But there's so much to think about,
the sturdy voice, the struggling young man, a garbage can blown
across the street, the woman who nods.

GAMES OF SURVIVAL

I remember my mother on lonely days, the gusto
with which she would get into the car, drive
to the driving range, shoot golf balls arcing
over the long green expanses, while Harold
her lover, worked, and how she loved his son's
horse, the stallion who couldn't race, and the
photo of her as an adolescent with raven hair,
pulling back the oars of the rowboat
on a glistening lake, how she still
comes to me at night, in dreams, advising
me on the many unnamed games of survival
I am poised to play.

DREAM OF A RIVER,
WILD HORSES

1.16.09

we were walking by a river
of clear running water, near
the ocean.

you were weeping.

wild horses went running
through the river, yet
we waded in the water
as the horses ran.

then the river bifurcated
and we kept walking in the water
near sand bars, dunes.

SHE HAS SAID ...

that she would be able to sing again, after the hoarseness subsides.

she has said that all belongs to the red shooting twig.

she will still mother, trembling in the car.

she's rocking gently.

she has said everything will turn out okay, and she hopes she is exactly perfectly correct.

the guitar responds to her fingers, a strong rhythmic cadence, and a lamentation.

About the Author

Judy Katz-Levine was born in Newark, New Jersey into a musical family. She graduated from Simmons College. Katz-Levine audited a course at M.I.T. with Denise Levertov, who was a great influence on her work. She has published two full-length collections of poetry—"When The Arms Of Our Dreams Embrace/Collected Poems" (SARU, 1991) and "Ocarina" (Tarsier/SARU, 2006). Her poems have appeared in "The Sun", "Fence", "Mother Jones", "Salamander", "The Plaza" (Japan)", "Origin 2008", "96 Inc.", "Istanbul Literary Review", "The Bitter Oleander", and myriad other magazines. She won a Massachusetts Cultural Council Grant in Poetry, and her poem "What I Didn't Know" was nominated for a Pushcart Prize.

Judy Katz-Levine is intensely influenced by jazz rhythms in her work, and by surrealist and expressionist poets and painters. She also has mystical leanings, and has gleaned much from the poems of Tagore, the stories of Rabbi Nachman of Breslov, and the "Tales Of The Chassidim" by Martin Buber.

Also a jazz flutist, Judy Katz-Levine sings in a choir, and lives with her husband, an acupuncturist and sax player.

OTHER TITLES FROM AHADADA

Ahadada Books publishes poetry. Preserving the best of the small press tradition, we produce finely designed and crafted books in limited editions.

Bela Fawr's Cabaret (David Annwn) **978-0-9808873-2-7**

Writes Gavin Selerie: "David Annwn's work drills deep into strata of myth and history,. exposing devices which resonate in new contexts. Faithful to the living moment, his poems dip, hover and dart through soundscapes rich with suggestion, rhythmically charged and etymologically playful. Formally adventurous and inviting disjunction, these texts retain a lyric coherence that powerfully renders layers of experience. The mode veers from jazzy to mystical, evoking in the reader both disturbance and content. *Bela Fawr's Cabaret* has this recognisable stamp: music and legend 'Knocked Abaht a Bit', mischievous humour yielding subtle insight."

Age of the Demon Tools (Mark Spitzer) **978-0-9808873-1-0**

Writes Ed Sanders: "You have to slow down, and absorb calmly, the procession of gritty, pointillist gnarls of poesy that Mark Spitzer wittily weaves into his book. Just the title, *Age of the Demon Tools*, is so appropriate in this horrid age of inappropriate technology—you know, corruptly programmed voting machines, drones with missiles hovering above huts, and mind reading machines looming just a few years into the demon-tool future. When you do slow down, and tarry within Spitzer's neologism-packed litanies, you will find the footprints of bards such as Allen Ginsberg, whose tradition of embedding current events into the flow of poesy is one of the great beacons of the new century. This book is worth reading if only for the poem 'Unholy Millenial Litany' and its blastsome truths."

Sweet Potatoes (Lou Rowan) **978-0-9781414-5-5**

Lou Rowan . . . is retired, in love and charged. He was raised by horse breeders and went to Harvard and thus possesses an outward polish. But he talks like a radical, his speech incongruous with his buttoned-down appearance. *Golden Handcuffs Review*, the local literary magazine that Rowan founded and edits, is much like the man himself: appealing and presentable on the outside, a bit wild and experimental at the core.

Deciduous Poems (David B. Axelrod) **978-0-9808873-0-3**

Dr. David B. Axelrod has published hundreds of articles and poems as well as sixteen books of poetry. Among his many grants and awards, he is recipient of three Fulbright Awards including his being the first official Fulbright Poet-in-Residence in the People's Republic of China. He was featured in Newsday as a "Star in his academic galaxy," and characterized by the New York Times as "a treat." He has shared the stage with such notables as Louis Simpson, X. J. Kennedy, William Stafford, Robert Bly, Allen Ginsburg, David Ignatow and Galway Kinnell, in performance for the U.N., the American Library Association, the Struga Festival, and hundreds more schools and public events. His poetry has been translated into fourteen languages and he is a frequent and celebrated master teacher.

Late Poems of Lu You (Burton Watson) **978-0-9781414-9-3**

Lu You (1125–1210) whose pen name was 'The Old Man Who Does as He Pleases,' was among the most prolific of Chinese poets, having left behind a collection of close to ten thousand poems as well as miscellaneous prose writings. His poetry, often characterized by an intense patriotism, is also notable for its recurrent expression of a carefree enjoyment of life. This volume consists of twenty-five of Burton Watson's new translations, plus Lu You's poems as they appear in the original, making this a perfect collection for the lay reader as well as for those with a mastery of Song dynasty Chinese.

Oulipoems (Philip Terry) **978-0-978-1414-2-4**

Philip Terry was born in Belfast in 1962 and has been working with Oulipian and related writing practices for over twenty years. His lipogrammatic novel *The Book of Bachelors* (1999), was highly praised by the Oulipo: "Enormous rigour, great virtuosity—but that's the least of it." Currently he is Director of Creative Writing at the University of Essex, where he teaches a graduate course on the poetics of constraint. His work has been published in *Panurge*, *PN Review*, *Oasis*, *North American Review* and *Onedit*, and his books include the celebrated anthology of short stories *Ovid Metamorphosed* (2000) and *Fables of Aesop* (2006). His translation of Raymond Queneau's last book of poems, *Elementary Morality*, is forthcoming from Carcanet. *Oulipoems* is his first book of poetry.

The Impossibility of Dreams (David Axelrod) **978-0-9781414-3-1**

Writes Louis Simpson: "Whether Axelrod is reliving a moment of pleasure, or a time of bitterness and pain, the truth of his poetry is like life itself compelling." Dr. David B. Axelrod has published hundreds of articles and poems as well as sixteen books of poetry. Among his many grants and awards, he is recipient of three Fulbright Awards including his being the first official Fulbright Poet-in-Residence in the People's Republic of China . He was featured in *Newsday* as a "Star in his academic galaxy," and characterized by the *New York Times* as "A Treat." His poetry has been translated into fourteen languages and he is a frequent and celebrated master teacher.

Now Showing (Jim Daniels) **0-9781414-1-5**

Of Jim Daniels, the *Harvard Review* writes, "Although Daniels' verse is thematically dark, the energy and beauty of his language and his often brilliant use of irony affirm that a lighter side exists. This poet has already found his voice. And he speaks with that rare urgency that demands we listen." This is affirmed by Carol Muske, who identifies the "melancholy sweetness" running through these poems that identifies him as "a poet born to praise".

China Notes & The Treasures of Dunhuang (Jerome Rothenberg) **0-9732233-9-1**

"*The China Notes* come from a trip in 2002 that brought us out as far as the Gobi Desert & allowed me to see some of the changes & continuities throughout the country. I was traveling with poet & scholar Wai-lim Yip & had a chance to read poetry in five or six cities & to observe things as part of an ongoing discourse with Wai-lim & others. The ancient beauty of some of what we saw played out against the theme park quality of other simulacra of the past....A sense of beckoning wilderness/wildness in a landscape already cut into to serve the human need for power & control." So Jerome Rothenberg describes the events behind the poems in this small volume—a continuation of his lifelong exploration of poetry and the search for a language to invoke the newness and strangeness both of what we observe and what we can imagine.

The Passion of Phineas Gage & Selected Poems (Jesse Glass) **0-9732233-8-3**

The Passion of Phineas Gage & Selected Poems presents the best of Glass' experimental writing in a single volume. Glass' ground-breaking work has been hailed by poets as diverse as Jerome Rothenberg, William Bronk and Jim Daniels for its insight into human nature and its exploration of forms. Glass uses the tools of postmodernism: collaging, fragmentation, and Oulipo-like processes along with a keen understanding of poetic forms and traditions that stretches back to Beowulf and beyond. Moreover, Glass finds his subject matter in larger-than-life figures like Phineas Gage—the man whose life was changed in an instant when an iron bar was sent rocketing through his brain in a freak accident—as well as in ants processing up a wall in time to harpsichord music in order to steal salt crystals from the inner lip of a cowrie shell. The range and ambition of his work sets it apart. The product of over 30 years of engagement with the avant-garde, *The Passion of Phineas Gage & Selected Poems* is the work of a mature poet who continues to reinvent himself with every text he produces.

Send a request to be added to our mailing list:
http://www.ahadadabooks.com/

Ahadada Books are available from these fine distributors:

Canada
Ahadada Books
3158 Bentworth Drive
Burlington, Ontario
Canada, L7M 1M2
Phone: (905) 617-7754
http://www.ahadadabooks.com

United States of America
Small Press Distribution
1341 Seventh Street
Berkeley, CA 94710-1409
Phone: (510) 524-1668
Fax: (510) 524-0852
http://www.spdbooks.org/

Europe
West House Books
40 Crescent Road
Nether Edge, Sheffield
United Kingdom S7 1HN
Phone: 0114-2586035
http://www.westhousebooks.co.uk/

Japan
Intercontinental Marketing Corp.
Centre Building 2nd floor
1-14-13 Iriya, Taitoku
Tokyo 110-0013
Telephone 81-3-3876-3073
http://www.imcbook.net/